CAT TO THE MOON

AMAZING CAT FACTS!!

In ancient Egypt some cats were made into mummies after they died. Sometimes mummies of mice were buried with them.

To Jack,
in celebration of his first year
—S.J.M.

The publisher and author would like to thank
teachers Patricia Chase, Phyllis Goldman, and
Patrick Hopfensperger for their help in making
the math in MathStart just right for kids.

We would also like to thank Linda Borcover
and her kittens, Louis and Martine,
for loaning us their journal.

HarperCollins®, ☕®, and MathStart® are registered trademarks of
HarperCollins Publishers. For more information about the
MathStart series, please write to HarperCollins Children's Books,
10 East 53rd Street, New York, NY 10022, or visit our web site at
http://www.harperchildrens.com. Bugs incorporated in the
MathStart series design were painted by Jon Buller.

PEPPER'S JOURNAL: A KITTEN'S FIRST YEAR
Text copyright © 2000 by Stuart J. Murphy
Illustrations copyright © 2000 by Marsha Lynn Winborn
Manufactured in China. All rights reserved.

Library of Congress Cataloging-in-Publication Data
Murphy, Stuart J., date
  Pepper's journal: a kitten's first year / by Stuart J. Murphy ; illustrated by
Marsha Lynn Winborn.
      p.   cm. — (MathStart)
  "Level 2, Reading calendars."
  Summary: Lisa keeps a journal of her new kitten's first year.
  ISBN 0-06-027618-5. — ISBN 0-06-027619-3 (lib. bdg.) — ISBN 0-06-446723-6
  (pbk.)
      [1. Diaries—Fiction.   2. Cats—Fiction.   3. Animals—Infancy—
Fiction.]   I. Winborn, Marsha, ill.   II. Title.   III. Series.
PZ7.M9563Ki   2000   98-47523
[E]—dc21   CIP
                                                                        AC

Typography by Elynn Cohen
5 6 7 8 9 10
❖

to: Ms. Vanore
and her student

MATH = FUN !

Stuart J. Murphy
2005

CATNIP

MathStart® CALENDARS

Pepper's Journal

A Kitten's First Year

by Stuart J. Murphy • illustrated by Marsha Winborn

HarperCollinsPublishers

LEVEL 2

"We're going to get a kitten!" said Joey. "Grandma says when Snowy has her kittens, we can keep the one we like best."

"Mom gave me this journal to record our kitten's first year. I can't wait to start writing!" said Lisa. "I wonder what day our kitten will be born."

MARCH 6

March 6 is my favorite day! Snowy had three perfect kittens this morning.

I checked out *every* book in the library about kittens. I read that newborn kittens can't hear or see. Their ears and eyes stay sealed for seven to ten days. Grandma told me that their supersoft fur won't even keep them warm yet. So all the kitties are snuggling close to Snowy.

WHEEEEEEEEE!

One book says kittens are born inside watery bubbles. WEIRD! Their mommies lick away the sacks so the kittens can breathe.

The kittens are so small, they weigh less than a **Candy bar** — even one that Joey has munched.

Kittens weigh about 3 ounces at birth.

YUM BAR

The MARCH cat is gentle, dreamy, and fascinated by water.

MARCH

Sun.	Mon.	Tue.	Wed.	Thurs.	Fri.	Sat.
			1	2	3	4
5	6	7	8	9	10	11
12	13	14	15	16	17 ST. PATRICK'S DAY	18
19	20	21	22	23	24	25
26	27	28	29	30	31	

MARCH 7

The kittens are already one day old. But Mom told us
we have to wait until the kittens are a week old before
we can visit them. Doesn't she know a week is seven looong days?

The kittens will be starting to
open their eyes then. Maybe I'll
be the first person my kitty sees!

6

1*day*old!!

DRINK UP! Every hour or so the kittens fill their tiny tummies with **Snowy's warm milk.** The kittens figure out where to nurse by using their sense of smell and their whiskers.

MARCH

Sun.	Mon.	Tue.	Wed.	Thurs.	Fri.	Sat.
			1	2	3	4
5	6	7	8	9	10	11
12	13	14	15	16	17 ST. PATRICK'S DAY	18
19	20	21	22	23	24	25
26	27	28	29	30	31	

MARCH 13

We finally met the kittens! They looked like bits of fluff with bright pink noses. Grandma said that the kittens don't like to be held yet, but she let me touch each one with the tip of my finger.

Snowy watched me every minute.

When the kittens are one month old—that's more than four weeks—we get to pick the one that we will keep.

Flat ears start to poke up.

Tiny eyes peek open!

Legs barely lift up bodies.

MARCH

Sun.	Mon.	Tue.	Wed.	Thurs.	Fri.	Sat.
			1	2	3	4
5	6	7	8	9	10	11
12	13	14	15	16	17 ST. PATRICK'S DAY	18
19	20	21	22	23	24	25
26	27	28	29	30	31	

AMAZING CAT FACTS!!

Cats nearly always land on their feet when they fall.

What a GREAT Magician I AM. LOOK...PRESTO-CHANGO!! This big ugly frog is now a sweet little kitty!

POOF!!

APRIL 6

The kittens grew so much in one month! Now they can see and hear just fine, and even walk. Or is it wobble? They weren't very shy, but the black-and-white kitten was the most frisky and friendly. Joey and I knew he was the one for us.

Joey said the little black spots on our kitten's white fur look like pepper. What a good name for our kitten! I can't believe Joey thought of it instead of me!

Now our kitty has the perfect name—

Pepper.

APRIL

Sun.	Mon.	Tue.	Wed.	Thurs.	Fri.	Sat.
						1
2	3	4	5	6	7	8
				13	14	15
16	17	18	19	20	21	22
23	24	25	26	27	28	29
30						

TODAY THE KITTIES ARE ONE MONTH OLD!!

Now the kittens are old enough to try solid food. In a couple more weeks they won't need Snowy's milk anymore.

BY JOEY

MAY 6

Pepper is two months old. That means we can bring him home today. There's so much to get ready! Mom helped me make a cozy bed. We cut up a cardboard box and put a soft, snuggly blanket in it. We still have to get a litter box, a scratching post, a carrier, combs, toys, bowls. . . . How can such a little kitten need such a lot of stuff?

Pepper will love these!

LITTER BOX

two months old!!

The MAY cat is patient and affectionate, and expects luxury.

MAY

Sun.	Mon.	Tue.	Wed.	Thurs.	Fri.	Sat.
	1	2	3	4	5	6
7	8	9	10	11	12	13
14 HAPPY MOTHER'S DAY	15	16	17	18	19	20
21	22	23	24	25	26	27
28	29	30	31			

TOP HAT CAT

GOOD STUFF!

PET CATALOG

THE NEWEST CAT BED!! WILL YOUR CAT EVER LEAVE IT??

SCRATCHIN POST ~

CAT CARRIER

JUNE 6

Today Pepper had his three-month checkup. The vet looked Pepper over from head to tail. Then she gave him a shot to keep him from getting sick. The vet told us all the ways to help Pepper grow into a healthy cat.

Pepper's toes have claws at the end of them. He can pull these claws under his skin when he wants to walk quietly. Or he can push them out when he wants to scratch or climb. Sometimes Pepper tests his claws on the curtains! Then I take him right over to his scratching post. Soon he'll learn that's the only place for clawing.

WHAT KITTY NEEDS

1. Lots of water
2. fresh litter
3. Exercise
4. sleep
5. Good food
6. Check-ups
7. LOVE!

The JUNE cat is lively, curious, and very expressive.

JUNE

Sun.	Mon.	Tue.	Wed.	Thurs.	Fri.	Sat.
				1	2	3
4	5	6	7	8	9 .	10
11	12	13	14	15 SCHOOL'S OUT!	16	17
18 HAPPY FATHER'S DAY	19	20	21	22	23	24
25	26	27	28	29	30	

Pepper was a Brave Kitty at the vet

BRAVE KITTY

JULY 20

Our summer camping trip started today. This year we brought Pepper.

I told spooky stories, but Joey got the biggest scare. When the beam of his flashlight hit Pepper's eyes, they glowed! Joey didn't know that all cats have "mirrors" in the backs of their eyes that reflect light and help cats see better when it's getting dark. Joey can be such a scaredy cat.

16

Pepper's eyelids keep his eyes from feeling dry. They spread tears just like teeny-tiny windshield wipers. He also has a third eyelid for extra protection.

Cats can't see in the dark, but they can see about 5 times better than people can in low light.

EEK!

The JULY cat is moody, sensitive, and a good provider.

JULY

Sun.	Mon.	Tue.	Wed.	Thurs.	Fri.	Sat.
						1
2	3	4 July 4th	5	6	7	8
9	10	11	12	13	14	15
16	17	18	19	20	21	22
23	24	25	26	27	28	29
30	31					

Pepper uses his eyes, ears, nose, and paws to explore. He rubs up against everything he sees. When he rubs against my legs, he is saying, "You belong to me!"

AUGUST 28

Pepper is the first one to know I'm home. That's because he can hear and smell better than people. He can also see better when there isn't much light. You can't sneak up on Pepper!

Pepper is such a smart kitten. He always wins at hide-and-seek— until we bring out the kitty treats.

SHAKE SHAKE

KITTY YUM

18

5 months,
3 weeks,
and **1** day old →

I can wiggle my ears a little bit, but Pepper can point his ears in the direction that a sound is coming from. He can move his ears together or one at a time. I wish I could do that!

Bzzzzzzz

AUGUST

Sun.	Mon.	Tue.	Wed.	Thurs.	Fri.	Sat.
		1	2	3	4	5
6	7	8	9	10	11	12
13	14	15	16	17	18	19
20	21	22	23	24	25	26
27	**28**	29	30	31		

LAST DAY OF SUMMER VACATION

Today I took Pepper to school for show-and-tell. Everyone loved Pepper so much that next week they're *all* bringing their pets—puppies, fish, birds, bunnies, mice, and even a snake. Good thing our teacher, Mrs. Connor, loves animals as much as we do!

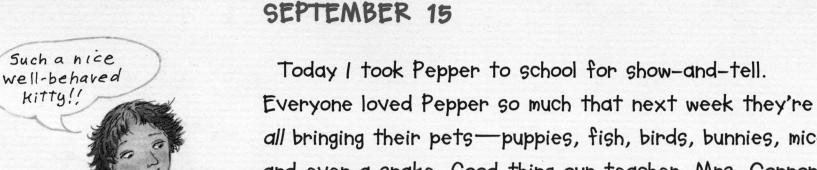

At school, I always hold my pencil like this.

And Pepper always plays with his toys like this!

We're both right-handed! Or is that right-pawed?

My books say, out of 10 cats, 4 would probably be right-pawed, 4 would be left-pawed, and the other 2 wouldn't use one paw more than the other.

The SEPTEMBER cat is simple, down-to-earth, and finicky.

SEPTEMBER

Sun.	Mon.	Tue.	Wed.	Thurs.	Fri.	Sat.
					1	2
3	4	5 1st day of School	6	7	8	9
10	11	12	13	14	15	16
17	18	19	20	21	22	23
24	25	26	27	28	29	30

OCTOBER 31
HALLOWEEN

Pepper helped me pick out the purr-fect Halloween costume for the Halloween party. We didn't win the contest, but I already had the best prize of all.

Pepper is almost ____ months old.

Pepper's **C**at-o-lantern

Pepper stays clean without ever using soap or water. His Tongue is covered with little hooks that pick all the dirt off his fur. Joey wishes he knew Pepper's Secret!

The OCTOBER cat is peaceful, lovable, and cooperative.

OCTOBER

Sun.	Mon.	Tue.	Wed.	Thurs.	Fri.	Sat.
1	2	3	4	5	6	7
8	9	10	11	12	13	14
15	16	17	18	19	20	21
22	23	24	25	26	27	28
29	30	**31**				

Happy Halloween

Lots of family came to visit on Thanksgiving! Of all the cousins, aunts, uncles, and grandparents, Pepper decided he liked our baby cousin Sam the best. Maybe it's because they're both eight months old. Or maybe he just liked playing with Sam's blanket.

When Pepper takes a drink, he curls his tongue like a cup and tosses drops of water to the back of his mouth. Once a puddle forms back there, Pepper swallows.

Pepper in Sneaks

I had to read Pepper's favorite story to him again. Won't he ever get tired of ?

PUSS IN BOOTS

The NOVEMBER cat is passionate, intense, and hard to ignore.

NOVEMBER

Sun.	Mon.	Tue.	Wed.	Thurs.	Fri.	Sat.
			1	2	3	4
5	6	7	8	9	10	11
12	13	14	15	16	17	18
19	20	21	22	**23**	24	25
26	27	28	29	30		

HAPPY THANKSGIVING

DECEMBER 9

Joey and I shopped all day for holiday presents. We thought it was going to take a long time to wrap them, but then Pepper helped us. And it took a very, very long time instead!

Pepper knows just how to handle the holiday Crazies— he takes a NAP! ZZZZZZ With all their napping, cats wind up sleeping 18 out of 24 hours. So when Pepper is 4 years old, he'll have spent about three years sleeping and one year awake!

by Joey

The DECEMBER cat is playful, optimistic, and a daring explorer.

DECEMBER

Sun.	Mon.	Tue.	Wed.	Thurs.	Fri.	Sat.
					1	2
3	4	5	6	7	8	9
10	11	12	13	14	15	16
17	18	19	20	21 HANUKKAH BEGINS	22	23
24	25 CHRISTMAS DAY	26	27	28	29	30
31 NEW YEAR'S EVE						

JANUARY 1
NEW YEAR'S DAY

Happy New Year! We fell asleep cuddling with Pepper last night and woke up in a whole new year.

Combing Pepper's fur is fun for me and good for him. This means that Pepper won't swallow so much hair when he washes himself.

PURRRRRRR!!!!

PEPPER'S FAVORITE JOKES

Q: How is a kitten like a penny?

A: Both have a head on one side and a tail on another. Ha!

Q: What kind of kitten lives in the ocean?

A: An octopus.

Q: What kind of kitten works at a hospital?

A: A first-aid kit.

The JANUARY cat is ambitious, determined, and an expert climber.

JANUARY

Sun.	Mon.	Tue.	Wed.	Thurs.	Fri.	Sat.
	1	2	3	4	5	6
7	8	9	10	11	12	13
14	15	16	17	18	19	20
21	22	23	24	25	26	27
28	29	30	31			

FEBRUARY 14 • VALENTINE'S DAY

It's Valentine's Day. That means Pepper's birthday is coming soon. He's almost one year old. I can't believe it takes only twelve months for a little ball of fuzz to turn into our own playful Pepper!

1 day

1 week

1 month

2 months

6 months

8 months

Almost
1 year

2 weeks and **6** days until PEPPER'S BIRTHDAY PARTY!

IT'S A PARTY!

INVITE: Grandma + Snowy + Joey + Mom

GIFT LIST: KITTY YUMS + ⚫ + 🐭

TREATS: Pepper can't eat cookies, but I think he'll still like what he sees....

ROSES ARE RED
VIOLETS ARE BLUE
Pepper, my
Kitty Cat
I
Love U!!
Lisa

The FEBRUARY cat is original and intellectual, and makes unusual friends.

FEBRUARY

Sun.	Mon.	Tue.	Wed.	Thurs.	Fri.	Sat.
				1	2	3
4	5	6	7	8	9	10
11	12	13	**14**	15	16	17
18	19	20	21	22	23	24
25	26	27	28			

I LOVE MY CAT

MARCH 6
PEPPER'S BIRTHDAY

Happy Birthday, Pepper!

The MARCH cat is gentle, dreamy, and fascinated by water.

MARCH

Sun.	Mon.	Tue.	Wed.	Thurs.	Fri.	Sat.
				1	2	3
4	5	6	7	8	9	10
11	12	13	14	15	16	17 ST. PATRICK'S DAY
18	19	20	21	22	23	24
25	26	27	28	29	30	31

PEPPER'S FIRST YEAR

JANUARY

Sun.	Mon.	Tue.	Wed.	Thurs.	Fri.	Sat.
						1
2	3	4	5	6	7	8
9	10	11	12	13	14	15
16	17	18	19	20	21	22
23	24	25	26	27	28	29
30	31					

FEBRUARY

Sun.	Mon.	Tue.	Wed.	Thurs.	Fri.	Sat.
		1	2	3	4	5
6	7	8	9	10	11	12
13	14	15	16	17	18	19
20	21	22	23	24	25	26
27	28	29				

MARCH

Sun.	Mon.	Tue.	Wed.	Thurs.	Fri.	Sat.
				1	2	3	4
5	6	7	8	9	10	11
12	13	14	15	16	17	18
19	20	21	22	23	24	25
26	27	28	29	30	31	

APRIL

Sun.	Mon.	Tue.	Wed.	Thurs.	Fri.	Sat.
2	3	4	5	6	7	8
9	10	11	12	13	14	15
16	17	18	19	20	21	22
23	24	25	26	27	28	29
30						

MAY

Sun.	Mon.	Tue.	Wed.	Thurs.	Fri.	Sat.
	1	2	3	4	5	6
7	8	9	10	11	12	13
14	15	16	17	18	19	20
21	22	23	24	25	26	27
28	29	30	31			

JUNE

Sun.	Mon.	Tue.	Wed.	Thurs.	Fri.	Sat.
			1	2	3
4	5	6	7	8	9	10
11	12	13	14	15	16	17
18	19	20	21	22	23	24
25	26	27	28	29	30	

JULY

Sun.	Mon.	Tue.	Wed.	Thurs.	Fri.	Sat.
						1
2	3	4	5	6	7	8
9	10	11	12	13	14	15
16	17	18	19	20	21	22
23	24	25	26	27	28	29
30	31					

AUGUST

Sun.	Mon.	Tue.	Wed.	Thurs.	Fri.	Sat.
	1	2	3	4	5
6	7	8	9	10	11	12
13	14	15	16	17	18	19
20	21	22	23	24	25	26
27	28	29	30	31		

SEPTEMBER

Sun.	Mon.	Tue.	Wed.	Thurs.	Fri.	Sat.
				1	2
3	4	5	6	7	8	9
10	11	12	13	14	15	16
17	18	19	20	21	22	23
24	25	26	27	28	29	30

OCTOBER

Sun.	Mon.	Tue.	Wed.	Thurs.	Fri.	Sat.
1	2	3	4	5	6	7
8	9	10	11	12	13	14
15	16	17	18	19	20	21
22	23	24	25	26	27	28
29	30	31				

NOVEMBER

Sun.	Mon.	Tue.	Wed.	Thurs.	Fri.	Sat.
		1	2	3	4
5	6	7	8	9	10	11
12	13	14	15	16	17	18
19	20	21	22	23	24	25
26	27	28	29	30		

DECEMBER

Sun.	Mon.	Tue.	Wed.	Thurs.	Fri.	Sat.
					1	2
3	4	5	6	7	8	9
10	11	12	13	14	15	16
17	18	19	20	21	22	23
24	25	26	27	28	29	30
31						

JANUARY

Sun.	Mon.	Tue.	Wed.	Thurs.	Fri.	Sat.
1	2	3	4	5	6
7	8	9	10	11	12	13
14	15	16	17	18	19	20
21	22	23	24	25	26	27
28	29	30	31			

FEBRUARY

Sun.	Mon.	Tue.	Wed.	Thurs.	Fri.	Sat.
			1	2	3
4	5	6	7	8	9	10
11	12	13	14	15	16	17
18	19	20	21	22	23	24
25	26	27	28			

MARCH

Sun.	Mon.	Tue.	Wed.	Thurs.	Fri.	Sat.
				1	2	3
4	5	6	7	8	9	10
11	12	13	14	15	16	17
18	19	20	21	22	23	24
25	26	27	28	29	30	31

In *Pepper's Journal*, the math concept is "calendar time." Understanding the relationships among days, weeks, months, and years is important in a child's daily life.

If you would like to have more fun with the math concepts presented in *Pepper's Journal*, here are a few suggestions:

• Read the story with the child and talk about what is going on in each picture.

• Ask questions throughout the story, such as: "How old is Pepper now?" "Which day is Pepper's birthday?" "How many months are in a year?"

• After reading the story, make a list of family events that occur on a weekly, monthly, and yearly basis. Help the child record the events on a calendar.

• Try these calendar puzzles to show that time is a continual process: If you know the first Wednesday in a month is on the 4th, can you predict what the date of the third Wednesday will be? If you know that a Monday is on the 11th of a month, what date will the next Friday be? What date follows January 31st? What is the date two weeks after April 25th?

Following are some activities that will help you extend the concepts presented in *Pepper's Journal* into a child's life:

Holidays: Make a time line of the various holidays the child's family celebrates over the course of a year. Have the child draw pictures of the celebrations or cut them out from a magazine. Count the number of days or weeks between holidays.

My First Year: Talk about the first year of the child's life. At what age did he or she first sit up? Talk? Start to crawl? Count the time in days or months between the events.

Calendar: Make your own calendar. Draw 12 blank grids (use the ones in *Pepper's Journal* as a guide) and work together to decorate each one. Staple the pages together and hang the calendar up for use all year long!

The following books include similar concepts to those that are presented in *Pepper's Journal*:

- THE VERY HUNGRY CATERPILLAR by Eric Carle
- CHICKEN SOUP WITH RICE by Maurice Sendak
- GINGERBREAD DAYS by Joyce Carol Thomas

PEPPER'S FIRST YEAR

PEPPER'S FIRST YEAR

33

PEPPER'S FIRST YEAR